CW00555030

PSYCHOLOGY OF RELATIONSHIPS:

THE SOCIAL PSYCHOLOGY OF FRIENDSHIPS, ROMANTIC RELATIONSHIPS, PROSOCIAL BEHAVIOUR AND MORE
THIRD EDITION

CONNOR WHITELEY

ACKNOWLEDGMENTS

Thank you to all my readers, without you I couldn't do what I love.

INTRODUCTION

Sometimes I think we all take a moment in friendships or romantic relationships to think about: "why are we, friends or partners?"

We've all been there.

Interestingly enough psychology can help us to answer this question because there are a lot of answers.

Whether it's a biological, psychological or social reason for relationships forming, psychology has an answer for you.

So this book will explain a wide range of explanations for why friendships and romantic relationships form.

However, this book won't stop there, because why do people help each other?

That's not clear.

Especially, when Altruism, a special kind of helping behaviour, can end up harming us?

So, this book will explore Bystanderism, Altruism and more.

Keep reading to learn more about this great topic!

Who is this Book For?

If you're a University student or someone interested in social psychology and the psychology of human relationships and you want a book that breaks content into interesting and easy to understand pieces of information. Then this is the book for you.

I won't give you long boring complex paragraphs filled with head-spinning information.

Instead, I'll give you lots of engaging information and I'll explain how this relates to everyday life.

In other words, this is the sort of textbook I would like for my degree. Engaging without compromising on the content.

Who Am I?

I always like to know who writes whatever nonfiction book I read.

So, in case you're like me I'm Connor Whiteley I'm an author of over 30 books and 11 of these are psychology books. Ranging in topics on biological psychology to Forensic Psychology to Clinical Psychology.

Also, I'm a university student at the University of Kent and I'm the host of the weekly The Psychology World Podcast where I talk about psychology news and a range of psychology topics.

Finally, I've interviewed New York Times and USA Today bestselling author J. F Penn as well.

So let's move onto the great topic of relationship psychology!

CHAPTER 1: WHY ARE RELATIONSHIPS IMPORTANT?

Human relationships are very important to humans because human relationships but especially close relationships; such as sexual relationships or relationships with close friends; are the centre of human existence.

We cannot thrive without them.

I know from personal experience that I prefer to have close relationships and the relationships I have had have been very important in my life and as humans, we have a fundamental need to affiliate (Baurester and Leary, 1995)

In other words, humans are a social species, so we need to be with others and humans are constantly thinking about affiliation, relationships and being with others.

Therefore, if humans have a lack of close

relationships; for example, if you have a lack of close friends or family or a lack of sexual relationships; then the following can happen:

- You can become depressed (See Abnormal Psychology for more information)
- You can feel alienated by society.
- You can become angry and aggressive.

Overall, close relationships are needed for survival and this can be clearly seen in our history because if close relationships weren't needed for survival. Then we could easily hunt alone for food as well as we could survive alone.

However, we know this to be false as we needed to form communities and societies to survive as well as we know that it's easier to hunt in packs.

Referring to modern times, this is still relevant as we often need close relationships to help us bring up our children. For instance, babysitting whilst we work or asking them to buy food for us so we don't need to bring the baby out into the cold.

Therefore, supporting the idea that close human relationships are needed for survival.

Finally, human relationships are vital for children to be successful in adulthood. For example, relationships with a sibling can determine how successful a child's relationships with others will be in the present or future.

Meaning that if a child has a bad relationship with their siblings then they are more likely to have bad relationships with others.

In addition, Bovers et al (1994) shows that school bullies are more likely to have bad relationships with their sibling compared to non-bullies. Consequently, showing the importance of positive sibling relationships.

Now that we know why human relationships are important, we can start to look at the causes...

PART ONE:
THE CAUSES OF
RELATIONSHIPS

CHAPTER 2: THE BIOLOGICAL CAUSES OF RELATIONSHIPS

There are many interesting reasons why relationships form but before we explore these explanations in the next three chapters.

Ask yourself one simple question: Why are you attracted to the person you are?

Whether you're currently dating or not. I urge you to really think about the why.

Personally, I believe that the biological reasons for why I am attracted to the people that I am are mainly due to physical appearance and neurochemical reasons.

Now that we've begun to think about the reasons behind our relationships. We can start to explore the biological explanations.

There are a few main biological reasons why we

feel attracted to someone.

These main reasons are:

- Evolutionary reason- this reason suggests that the reason why humans find others attracted has evolved over time. To help with the survival of the species. We will explore this reason in a later case study.
- Genetic explanation- this reason is connected to evolutionary theory because with the two reasons together. They form an explanation for relationships. Were relationships could be caused by biological markers that signal compatibility with one another.
- Neurochemical explanation- this explanation involves the role of hormones and neurotransmitters in the role of relationships. This will be explored more in a study later. (Refer to Biological Psychology for more information)

Therefore, I have given you a quick look at how biology can cause relationships.

I would suggest checking out Biological Psychology if you haven't already because it will explain evolution, genetics and neurochemicals in a lot more depth.

Physical Appearance:

It is common sense that the more attractive you are the more likely you are to get dates (Berscheid et al, 1971) however there are other benefits to being physically attractive. For example, you tend to get better marks at university (Mandy and Sigail, 1974) and you are more likely to be successful in job interviews (Dipboye et al, 1977)

From where I stand I would love to be more attractive to get better in these job interviews.

Overall, by being physically attractive people automatically subscripted to the physical appearance stereotype which is associated with other socially desirable characteristics that leads to these other positive outcomes. As a result of this stereotype, this becomes self-fulfilling.

For instance: if your employer thinks that you are attractive then they will think that you have other desirable characteristics leading you to become more successful in a job interview then because you believe that you have these other characteristics. Then these characteristics like communications skills will improve. All because you believe that you have these characteristics.

I do love the mind and psychology.

Interestingly, average faces are more attractive.

(Halberstadi et al (2005)

Which I personally find very interesting because you would have thought that perfect or very attractive faces would be rated as more attractive, but this links into a lot of other topics but people prefer real people instead of posh, fake humans.

Although, it must be mentioned that being physically attractive isn't always good for a few reasons. Including stalking.

Linking to Culture:

On a quick final note about physical appearance, between different cultures and within cultures themselves. There is a wide variation but there's a lot of agreement that physical attractiveness is important in human relationships. (Langlosis and Roggman, 1990)

Note: it must be said that you do not need to be extremely physically attractive to be able to find love or find close relationships. Just be yourself and you will be fine.

Evolution:

Before we move into our first study, let's explore why evolution is involved in human relationships.

Facial symmetry is linked to the evolutionary explanation for human relationships because having a more symmetrical face shows:

- You have a wider gene pool which is ideal for reproduction.
- You are a stronger better mate,
- You're more fertile.

Lastly, people rate symmetrical faces as healthier, cleverer and extroverted as well as in society these features are deemed as better. Making you more likely to get dates or form relationships.

With the theory done, we can start to look at some studies.

This first study looked at the evolutionary explanation.

Buss (1989):

Over 10,000 people from 33 countries on 6 continents answered a questionnaire on mate preferences. Like: the number of children as well as a section on rating 18 characteristics to see how desirable they would be in a mate.

Results show:

- Females valued good financial prospect in a mate so that the females can maximise the survival chances of the offspring.

- Males preferred physical attractiveness because attractiveness is linked to fertility. Which is desirable.
- Males prefer mates who are younger because younger mates tend to be more fertile.
- Females prefer older mates because they tend to be more mature and wealthier. This increases survival chances of the offspring and thus the species.

In conclusion, results are consistent across all cultures and fit well with the evolutionary explanation.

Overall, males look for fertile females and females look to maximise reproductive success by looking for resources for self and offspring.

Critical Thinking:

A positive of the study is that it's a cross-cultural study. Meaning that we can see if this behaviour is universal and consistent with all cultures.

However, this study didn't use the same number of people from each country. Therefore, it's hard to use the sample to represent the whole of the country in terms of their cultural reasons for relationships. For example: in Iran, they used only 55 people compared to 1,491 in the USA.

Fisher, Aron and Brown (2005)

In this experiment, they got 17 people who reported themselves as 'intensely in love' and did a brain scan on them in an fMRI (functional Magnetic Resonance Imaging- further information in Biological Psychology) and got them to do some tasks.

Firstly, the participants got to look at a photo of a loved one for 30 seconds, then for 40 seconds they were required to count back from a number, for the next 30 seconds they got to look at an image of an emotionally neutral friend and for the last 20 seconds, they counted back again. They repeated this six times for a total of 720 seconds.

The results showed that when looking at the photo of the loved one there was increased activity in the dopamine; a neurotransmitter involved in the feelings of romantic love; rich areas of the brain. More specifically in the Ventral Tegmental Area which is apart of the so-called dopaminergic pathway. This is a reward system for pleasure and motivation in the brain.

In conclusion, the neurotransmitter dopamine is involved in the feelings of romantic love.

Critical Thinking:

The study was effectively designed so that the counting back exercise allowed the brain's activity to go back to 'normal' before the showing of each type of photo. Thus, this allowed the increase in brain activity to be clearly linked to the type of photo being shown.

Nevertheless, how can we be sure that those dopamine-rich areas of the brain only release dopamine? Is it possible that they release smaller amounts of other neurotransmitters and it's, in fact, the combination of this cocktail that creates the feelings of romantic love?

What do you think?

CHAPTER 3: COGNITIVE CAUSES OF RELATIONSHIPS

Now that we understand how our biology can cause us to feel attraction for someone or form other relationships. We can start to look at the psychological or mental reasons why we find people attractive as well as form other types of relationships.

In the cognitive realm of relationships, there are two main theories for relationships.

The first theory that we'll look at is the similarity-attraction hypothesis. This states that people form a relationship because they are similar to one another.

For example, think about your friend and you'll probably find that you're friends with them because you have things in common with them. Such as music preference, common interest and TV interests.

One personal example is that I and one of my friends have many common interests that are the foundation of our friendship. Such as scouting, sailing, opinions/attitudes and many more…

A study that supports this hypothesis is:

Byrne (1961):

Subjects were asked to rate several issues on their importance. Ranging from western films to premarital sex to music.

Then two weeks later they were shown a fake questionnaire. It was fake so one of four results could happen. Same on the important issues, same on the unimportant issues, opposite to the subject completely and the same as the subject on all issues.

Then they were asked to rate the attractiveness of the stranger based on their answers.

Results showed that more positive ratings were associated with a similar attitude as well as associated with similarity in important issues.

Critical Thinking:

The study has strong internal validity; they measured what they intended to measure; because the study effectively showed that attraction to the stranger was because they had more in common with them. This supports the hypothesis.

However, this study has low ecological validity;

can you apply the findings to the real world; because in the real world nobody meets people and rates them on the basis of a questionnaire. Even people on dating websites tend to be shown pictures and other information that impacts on their rating of attractiveness.

Consequently, to improve the experiment another research method could be used to support the findings and add creditability to the study. For example, interviews to see if their ratings were down to similarities or another reason.

Matching Hypothesis:

The next major cognitive theory for the formation of personal relationships is the matching hypothesis.

This hypothesis states that we are more likely to be attracted to someone who is equally socially desirable.

One way to think about this hypothesis is that your current or past partner according to the hypothesis is about the same as you in terms of how socially desirable they are.

For example, a popular person would date a popular person, as well as a person of average attractiveness, would date an equally average person.

And so on…

Although, people can compensate for a potential difference by making up for this difference in other areas. For instance:

- Wealth
- Sense of humour
- Good social care

This makes perfect sense I think because in terms of social desirability a person that I wanted to date in the past was different, but we would have made up for it through other factors. Such as we both matched our sense of humour and a lot of our interests matched, so that's another way to think about it.

The matching hypothesis/ principle can be done through asset matching as well.

This is where you are looking to match what you have with someone else and one method of doing this asset matching is through advertising. Such as attractive 28-year old seeking professional man.

I know it's not the social norm but it happens.

A study that supports the hypothesis is:

Berscheid et al (1971):

- Subjects were split into High Probability of rejection and low POR
- High POR got to meet their dates before the dance to either reject or accept them.
- Low POR was told that their dates agreed to go with whoever was chosen for them by the computer programme.
- Results showed that attractive subjects choose equally popular and attractive dates compared to High POR who choose more unattractive dates.
- As this was not different in the two groups increasing fear of rejection doesn't affect the choosing strategy.
- In conclusion, the matching principle may be a determinant of initial contact but not of maintaining already established relationships.

Critical Thinking:

A positive of this study is that it can be reproduced therefore future studies can repeat the experiment to test the results. This is positive because it adds creditability to the study if the results are the same or similar.

On the other hand, this study has low temporal validity; how time affects the results; because in this modern age of online dating and the crazy world of dating. It's possible that the results would be different as the computer programmes that had chosen the dates for the two groups could be more reliable or choose different dates for the two groups. Using more modern programmes to calculate the best match for the person.

Emotion:

Rather unsurprisingly emotion is something that is important for all human relationships and maybe it's not love.

Nonetheless, emotion will be involved to some degree or another as well as positive feelings lead to positive evaluation and vice versa. (Bryne, 1977)

Meaning that if you have positive feelings towards someone then this will lead to evaluating someone else as positive.

Like, I had positive feelings about a person at school and after talking to them. This leads me to evaluate them in a positive manner. Increasingly the likelihood of me talking to them again and forming a friendship. This friendship did happen.

Of course, when I discuss positive evaluations nobody actually sits there and thinks "Right let's make a list of the pros and cons of that person I met… okay there are more pros than cons so I'll see them again'

I mean that we evaluate them both unconsciously and conscious even if it is only a quick thought. Like: when you think "God that conversation was long" or "Wow she was interesting I think I'll definitely talk to her again"

Emotion or feelings towards someone can be direct; so you could possibly feel your attraction because of their physical appearance; or indirectly. For example, your feelings are not caused by that person.

An example of this emotional directionality from psychology research is Dutton and Aron (1974) were they got participants to walk across a shaky bridge with a male or female experimenter at the end of the bridge. The shakiness of the bridge caused arousal and after the participant got to the end of the bridge the experimenters would pass them a questionnaire with their phone number on it. The idea being that when the experimenter was a female the male would transfer their excitement; the arousal; to the female and be more likely to call the female experimenter than the male experimenter. The results confirmed this idea and the effect is called Excitation Transfer.

Overall, showing you that emotion can be indirect as in this study the emotion wasn't caused by the female experimenter. It was caused by the shaky bridge.

Equally, an example from my own life where this happened is that most of the people who I have been sexually interested in I have felt strong feelings for them caused by their physical attractiveness and personality. This is an example of direct emotions.

Whereas, my friendships; which are classed as relationships; have been caused by both direct and indirect feelings. For example, one friendship that I had that was caused by people talking about them positively so by the time I met them. I already liked them so after we got talking. We quickly became friends.

I know that this is a mixture of direct and indirect feelings, but I still strongly believe that the indirect feelings helped the friendship to form.

Attitudes and Similarity:

In relationships, the similarity of attitudes, interests and values are important.

If you think about it you'll probably find that you, your partner and friends, past partners as well as friends or people that you would like to have a relationship will probably have similar attitudes.

For instance: I and my friend had many similar attitudes towards certain things. Some of our similar attitudes included opinions of certain people, favourite food, world views, self-views and many more.

In fact, Galton (1970, 1952) found that wives and husbands are more similar than would occur via chance.

Therefore, supporting the idea that people in relationships are drawn together due to their similarity in attitudes.

What do you think?

Additionally, Festinger (1964) states that taking part in social comparison; where we compare each other to others; in relationships is one way to validate our own attitudes and beliefs. (See Social Psychology for more information)

We do this in relationships to make ourselves feel good.

We all have done this sort of comparison to our friends, family or loved ones.

I have done this before when I used to compare myself to one of my friends in terms of their quality of friendships and the quantity that they had as they seem to have more friends than myself.

However, I forget that I had what I needed. I had friends and that was what I needed.

Thus, showing how we compare ourselves with people we are in relationships with.

(I'll explain this concept more as well as the pros and cons of social comparison in Social psychology)

Going back to similarity, sometimes we seek or prefer complementary personalities, values or other things instead of similarities.

For Example:

> • A serious person might like to have a funny person around.
> • A very liberal person might like to have a more conservative person around.
> • A risk-taker might like to have someone who is more risk aversive around to keep them grounded.

A personal example of this in my own life is that a past friendship involved myself and another boy who was the perfect complement to myself as we still had a lot in common, but we both had different complimenting characteristics. Such as I thought things through and he didn't, he was very fun whilst I was only fun and more.

Overall, complementary characteristics can lead to liking yet in general, birds of a feather flock together.

Nonetheless going back to my friend, a lot of people thought that we will complete opposites so they couldn't understand why we were such great friends. This brings us to another interesting piece of psychological knowledge, where people can appear opposite but in fact, they can be similar in fundamental ways.

For me and my friend, we were fundamentally the same when it came to our thoughts on people, the world and other matters that we both deemed as important.

On the other hand, complementary characteristics are especially important in relationships that are a 'fling' but these relationships don't last long.

Reciprocity Principle:

Finally, an important cognitive reason for why relationships form is the reciprocity principle. This is where we like people who like us.

This I think we can all say is generally true as most of our friendships started because we liked another person. Subsequently, you'll probably find that because you liked them. This probably led to them liking you. Thus, forming a relationship or forming some sort of foundation, at least.

CHAPTER 4: SOCIAL CAUSES OF RELATIONSHIPS

Social explanations for why we form relationships. This is surely the most straightforward of the three reasons that we've looked at, and you would be correct.

As a quick-thinking exercise, make a quick mental list about why you could be attracted to someone. (Remember that we're looking at social reasons)

Here's my list:

- Proximity
- Popularity
- Social proof
- How familiar you are with someone

It would be interesting to see your list because I found it quite hard to make that list as my thoughts were mainly cognitive or biological.

There are a few social factors that cause relationships to form and this chapter aims to explore these reasons in more depth.

Familiarity:

This explanation is reasonably simple to understand because humans tend to like what we know. Whilst at first this seems false if you think about it but generally speaking, we do tend to form relationships with what we know.

The simplest example of this is that we tend to date within ethnic groups (Lui et al, 1995) as we are more familiar with our own ethnicity.

Another example is that humans tend to form relationships with people they know- as explained in more detail later in the chapter.

In fact, we are very picky about the familiarity concept as we prefer faces that look similar to ours. (Little and Perrett, 2002)

This I do have to laugh at as it makes us seem very particular when it comes to our mates and friends, and I can imagine the following comedy scene:

"Hi, do you want to be my friend?"

"No sorry, your face is too different to mine,"

Mere Exposure Effect:

Furthermore, familiarity is linked to the mere exposure effect where people like things merely because we are familiar to them.

This again is evident in everyday life through our bombardment of advertising and everyday life experience.

One example of this effect would be to imagine that you are given the choice of drinking two bottles of diet coke. One of them is from Coca Cola and the other is from Asia with a name that you're never heard of before.

Chances are that you would choose to drink the Coca Cola because you are more familiar with it.

Another example linking to human relationships is that you had to pick from two partners to go on a date with and the first person you had seen at school or work and they always looked kind but you never spoke to them before, then the other option was a person who you had never seen before.

Again, chances are that you would have picked the first person because you have been exposed to them.

In addition, if you can anticipate future

interaction then you tend to like them more. This has happened to me before because currently I'm living at university and as I know that I will be seeing my university flatmates more over the next year then I do tend to like them more.

However, as I know that after this year, I won't be seeing them again; there's no anticipation of future interaction; then I'm not trying as hard to form long-lasting relationships with them.

Nevertheless, I will attempt to keep in contact with two of the eight flatmates. Therefore, the future interaction fact depends on the personal situation.

Lastly, when the initial reaction is negative; for example, you meet your friend's boyfriend or girlfriend and they insult you immediately; then repeated exposure tends to lead to decreased liking.

A personal example of when this happened to me is that at university when I first met one of my flatmates, we got talking and he said that he wanted to be an author so I was talking to him about the author life and that it's the best time to be an author.

However, he started to say that I would never be successful and I would become a failure.

Therefore, I was a bit surprised because that's not something that you say to someone. Let alone the first time that you meet them.

Afterwards, whenever he would come into the kitchen I would dislike him a bit more because of he was just draining. But I am very civil to him and I have been trying to help him with his dream of becoming a writer but… he's in denial about the opportunities available now and in the future for authors.

Overall, because of that negative first interaction I dislike him and the more I'm exposed to him, the more I dislike him.

Proximity:

This refers to how close you are to someone in a physical space.

For example, you could become good friends with the person you work next to at work, or you could become friends with the person you sit next to in class.

As a result of you being close to them physically.

This has happened to me personally in my secondary or middle school when I sat next to this boy for a few weeks and we quickly became good friends.

In addition, when you are in close proximity to someone; let's take the class example; this can lead to familiarity.

Familiarity leads to relationships because you are more likely to like someone who you are familiar with compared to someone who you have no experience with.

Putting this example into context would be after you sit next to the person in class for a few weeks. You would be familiar with them and you would get talking to them so you would get to know them as well as be familiar with them.

Possibly leading to friendship.

This study demonstrates the point effectively.

Festinger, Schachter and Back (1950):

They studied residents of a large apartment complex where residents didn't choose where to live.

They were asked to indicate who they were friends within the complex.

Results showed that 41% of residents were friends with their next-door neighbours.

22% were friends with people who lived two doors away.

10% of people were friends with others who lived on the opposite side of the hall.

Critical Thinking:

This study has potentially high ecological validity; how you can apply the results to the general population; because the study was done in a real-world setting as well as it used real people. Therefore, the study shows the effects of proximity in the real world effectively.

However, this study could be outdated (low temporal validity) because this study was done before the creation of social media. Thus, social media could change the results for many reasons. One example could be that the people in the complex have several Facebook friends that are in the building as well, and as a result of their social media friendship, there might not be as significant of a difference in the data.

Digital Proximity:

However, in today's modern society many modern relationships are not dependent on physical proximity. Like social networks and a group of friends.

For example, a lot of my author friends are online.

The most obvious example of digital proximity is online dating.

Nonetheless, there are massive problems with

online relationships. Including, people can conceal pieces of themselves they don't like. (Whatty and Joinson, 2008) and increased time online is associated with feelings of depression and loneliness (Kraut et al, 1998)

Social Proof:

Social proof is when we are more likely to be attracted to someone who is well-accepted into society.

The study we're going to be looking at demonstrates the point very well so there's no real reason for me to talk more anymore.

Jones et al (2007):

Females were shown a picture of a male and asked to rate his attractiveness.

Later were shown the pair of photos again but this time one of the pictures had a woman looking at the man with a smile or neutral expression. They were asked to rate the attractiveness again.

Results showed that the second round of pictures rating didn't change for the photos that didn't have a woman staring at the man.

They did increase when a woman is smiling at the man.

They were lower for the woman staring at the man with a neutral expression.

Critical Thinking:

The study was well controlled as it showed the photos of the men alone and then later with the smile or neutral expressions. This allowed the researchers to effectively see if the expressions made a difference as the researcher had the participants baseline ratings of the men.

Nevertheless, the study could potentially lack ecological validity due to this isn't how women rate attractiveness in the real world. As when you see a man in the real world you would judge him on other things then looks, even if you don't realise it. For example body language, social cues or even who he's with and how he dresses.

Consequently, if the experiment was done in a natural setting the results could be different as this factor could play a role in the women's ratings of the men.

Culture:

Firstly, as mentioned in previous chapters as well as in other books in An Introductory Series, culture is very important in psychology let alone in terms of romantic love. As western cultures place a very high value on romantic love whereas in the East arranged marriages are the norm to some extent.

Furthermore, even in the Western world historically arranged marriages served society well.

Interestingly, people in arranged marriages rated that attraction for the other person increased over time.

The possible reasons for this increase in attraction can be linked to a lot of what has been mentioned in previous chapters as well as many aspects of humans are universally deemed universally attractive. For instance: politeness and being a physically attractive person. (Wheeler and Kin, 1997)

The list of cultural differences is endless when it comes to physiological appearance between cultures. (Perrett, 2010) and a very obvious example of this is that in some tribes of African they find girls with filed teeth girl attractive whereas in western society we do not.

Note: it is important not to judge cultures immediately when we encounter cultural differences between ours and their culture. It's important to learn the facts first about their reasoning behind it and then we can make an informed judgement.

Additionally, it must be said that different cultures have different social factors that can impact the likelihood of a relationship forming.

One particular social factor that is important in eastern cultures is family approval so this can be classed as an important determinant of attraction as if a family is unlikely to approve of this relationship; most typically referring to a romantic relationship; then it's unlikely that the relationship will form.

On the other hand, whilst this is more important in collectivistic cultures. This need for family approval can be seen in western societies as well because whether it's through a social network or Hollywood films western societies still hear about forbidden love that is subject to family disapproval.

Although, this isn't exclusive of romantic relationships as this can most certainly apply to friendships. As a result, everyone or at least most people have a friend that their parents or greater society would say that they should avoid.

This happened to me with a friendship as my parents (family disapproval) and many people said that I shouldn't be friends with him, and I need to avoid him. Leaving me to feel a bit sad in a way that I wasn't supported by many in this important friendship, so this did inhibit the friendship a little.

Nonetheless, over time they did begin to understand him, so the family approval increase allowing the friendship to blossom even more.

Therefore, the story shows that family disapproval can impact friendships as well but I hope that this little anecdote shows anyone who is facing a similar problem that things can get better.

PART TWO: COMMUNICATION, ATTRACTION & RELATIONSHIP BREAKDOWN

CHAPTER 5: COMMUNICATION IN RELATIONSHIPS

Communication- arguably one of the most important aspects of having a good relationship because bad communication can lead to fights, arguments and ultimately relationship breakdown.

I know from personal experience that communication is vital for positive relationships because I remember one example of poor communication. Where I and my friend had a rough patch because I perceived him as blanking me and not talking to me.

However, he wasn't and he was going through some stuff apparently, so his bad communication with me led to our relationship to become a bit negative. As a result of him not clearly communicating what he was doing. Leaving me to draw my own conclusion.

Theories of Communication:

Stepping away from common knowledge as well as my own personal stories about communication in relationships. There are a few theories that explore the science behind communication in relationships.

Social penetration theory was proposed by Altman and Taylor (1973) and it claims that a relationship moves from a shallow level of communication to a more intimate one. Intimacy is characterised by greater self-disclosure.

Personally, I love this theory because I believe it to be completely true because I can think of hundreds of personal stories were because I have told people very personal things. I and they have grown a lot closer.

I can think about one example that happened a few months ago where I told a friend something and because I told them something very personal. Our friendship became very closer almost to a brotherly-ish bond.

Can you think of any examples were because you told someone something you became closer?

Sheldon (2009):

243 undergraduate students were asked a series of questionnaires based on the person they talk to the most on Facebook.

Results show that the perception of attraction drives self-disclosure especially with the number of topics discussed with the person.

Increased disclosure was associated with less uncertainty about the person and this led to a sense of greater trust.

This supports uncertainty reduction theory because as people talk with others, they experience less uncertainty and are more likely to like each other.

Critical Thinking:

A positive of this study is that it has a large sample size because it uses over 200 students. As a result of this, we can apply the findings to a large number of people if not a whole population because the findings are supported by a large amount of data.

Equally, this sample is biased because the experiment only used one type of population or person in the study. The student population. As a result of this, it's hard to apply the findings to other populations. Such as adults, retired people and other cultures because we only have data from the student population.

Therefore, we can state the findings could apply to everyone but we wouldn't have proof to support that claim.

Attribution Theory:

This theory states that people are naïve psychologists that try to figure out the behaviour of others in order to make the social world more predictable and easier to navigate.

For instance, if you have ever seen someone doing something *abnormal* or *strange* in the street then it's natural for you to wonder why they are behaving like that.

Stratton (2003):

Stratton analysed films of 8 families that were in family therapy sessions.

All observations were coded using an attribution behavioural checklist. The total number of behaviour was 1,799.

Results showed that parents used attribution which implied that their children caused bad outcomes.

Parents made more dispositional; personality-based; attributions for their children than themselves.

Negative behaviours of children were described as more controllable than the parents.

In conclusion, these troubled families used a blaming attribution style that used blaming the children for negative outcomes. Therefore, we can see how distress in these families is caused by negative attribution.

Critical Thinking:

One positive of the study is that it has potentially high temporal validity because the study was done reasonably recently so the findings can still apply to today's society.

However, the study used families in therapy meaning that they were experiencing extreme difficulties as people use therapy as a last resort. Therefore, we can't say if the blaming attributions cause as much distress in a 'normal' family or a family not in therapy as we don't have data on 'normal' families.

CHAPTER 6: TYPES AND THEORIES OF ATTRACTION

In psychology, there are many theories behind the psychology of close relationships and some of these theories are very interesting. As we'll explore in this chapter as well as some you automatically think are true. Subsequently, there are others that cause you to question why YOU are in a relationship.

When I first had this lecture at University, when we explored some of these theories, I heard a few whispers of panic and questioning as if it was like a veil of blindness that had been lifted from the eyes of the young loved up students.

Social Exchange Theory

Our first theory is called: Social Exchange Theory.

This is one of my favourite theories because I believe it to be largely true and this theory has gained a lot of research support in recent years.

Therefore, the theory states that we are attracted to people because they offer us more rewards than others. (Thaibaut and Kelley, 1959)

In its most basic form, the theory is about costs and benefits.

Does the person I am with offer me more benefits than costs based on my previous experiences?

Some examples of benefits could include:

- Sex
- A shoulder to cry on
- Support
- Love and affection
- A great companion
- Fun
- Laughter

Some examples of the cost could be:

- Needy
- Arguments
- Stress

Overall, the fundamental question that the theory asks is: can we get a better relationship elsewhere?

Equity Theory:

Whilst, the last theory states that people actually want things from a relationship- this theory states that people want fairness rather than what they can get. (Hatfeild et al, 1978)

In other words, we like to be equal in the relationship.

Personally, this does make sense because nobody wants to be lesser in a relationship, so the idea of equality makes perfect sense. Especially, in this modern era.

However, if this theory is true in the strictest of senses then surely if you and your partner were equal but didn't have any benefits then the relationship would survive. Yet I doubt this idea?

As a result, I believe that both theories need to be combined in order to get to the *truth* as in the relationships I have seen. I think it's reasonable to think that people want both benefits to being with someone and they want equality in a relationship.

What do you think?

Balance Theory:

This theory states that in relationships we seek a balance and that a balance is important to relationship success as when people share similar attitudes. They are likely to reach a positive emotional state.

Whereas when people have dissimilar attitudes this can lead to negative emotions and as discussed later in the book relationship breakdown can occur.

Resulting in a need to restore balance or underlying differences between the individuals.

Types of Love:

There is no one type of love and that's what we will start to explore in this next section.

Passionate Love:
Firstly, there is passionate love.

This is most commonly seen in young people who are still exploring, developing and learning what love means.

Passionate love involves:

- Intense feelings
- Uncontrollable thoughts
- A deep longing for the other person
- Physiological responses (For example, an erection)
- The feeling of being in love

Companionate Love:

In addition, one of the other types of love is companionate love.

Companionate Love Involves:

- Deep, secure feeling (Hatfield, 1987)
- Unfrenzied
- Common in relationships that were once passionate.

I have an interesting thought about this type of love. I know that this type of love is meant to be for sexual relationships, but could this apply to close friends?

As you hear people mention that they love their friends and if you think about what companionate love involves; minus the last one; then there could be a link.

Maybe it's an idea for future research.

Sternberg's (1988) Theory Of Love

The Triangular Theory of Love: This is another theory that I quite like because in psychology I love/prefer theories to be holistic and focus on multiple factors.

Consequently, when I learnt that this theory focuses on the different types of love as well as the interaction between different factors to produce a behaviour. Needless to say, I instantly became interested.

The theory argues that 'love' is the result of the combination of passion, intimacy and commitment.

The theory states the type of love depends on the interaction between these concepts or factors.

Such As:

- Intimacy and passion gives you romantic love.

- Intimacy and commitment gives you companion love.

- Commitment and passion gives you fatuous love.

Looking at the theory, I think that it makes sense because as previously spoken about companion love doesn't tend to have passion in it but the people in this type of love are still intimate and committed to one another.

Although, I think something that could be added to the theory is a type of love that encompasses all three factors as I have seen and I like to think that in a relationship I would be passionate, committed and intimate with someone. Yet the theory states that that wouldn't happen, so that's something to consider if the theory gets reviewed or updated.

Types of Love:

In total according to Sternberg, there are 6 types of love but we're only going to look at three.

The Three Types of Love Include:

- Eros- passionate love which is all-consuming and in this type of relationship sex is very important as well as the idea of 'love at first sight' is common.
- Ludus- this is a type of love were the love or relationship is a game so the lovers are more interested in the number of relationships instead of the quality. These types of lovers see commitment as a trap, so infidelity is common.
- Mania- this type of love is intense, but these types of lovers are possessive, jealous and insecure. As a result, sex is all about assuring themselves or each other that their love is, for lack of a better term, real and not a made-up fantasy.

CHAPTER 7: MAINTAINING RELATIONSHIPS

Maintaining Relationships:

Once a relationship has been forged, it must be maintained.

Otherwise, it will start to rot and die.

That is a simple truth.

In fact, I am sorry to say that a lot of relationships are dead because I haven't really kept in good contact with some friends as I have grown and changed as a person.

Anyway, some methods that I use or used to keep in contact with friends and family include:

- Texting
- Calling
- Going out to the cinema

- Going out for a meal
- Having conversations

Generally, going out and seeing them.

Returning to the psychology part of the maintenance of relationships, all relationships need commitment as if you are not committed to your friends then the friendships dies. As well as if we lack commitment to our romantic partners then the relationship will breakdown as discussed in the next chapter.

Commitment can be defined as:

- Dedication to partner or friend
- Positive attraction to partner or friend

Interestingly, commitment is built on the belief that leaving the relationship; we'll be focusing on romantic relationships here; will be too costly to leave.

Some perceived positives of leaving a relationship could be:

- Freedom
- Independence
- Less financial burden
- Ability to see friends more

Generally, freedom is an overarching theme here as least from what I've witnessed in my life.

Especially, as the majority of my friends have said that it's great being single because you can do whatever you want.

Nonetheless, some negatives could be:

- Loneliness
- no emotional support
- no sex
- no love

As you can see commitment is about weighing up the pros and cons of leaving a relationship.

Resultbult's (1983) Investment Model of Commitment:

As with everything in psychology there has to be a model for it as psychologists do love a good model so without further a due I welcome you to the Investment Model of Commitment!

The model states that commitment is a combination of satisfaction, a lack of alternatives and incentives.

Personally, this model makes sense because it's logical to presume that commitment is made up of these things.

Let's look at an example of a romantic relationship to investigate this model.

Reasons for Satisfaction:

- The Sex.
- The Company.
- The Attention.
- The Disclosure.
- The Emotional Support.

Reasons for Possible Lack of Alternatives:

- No one else understands me like they do.
- No one else supports or loves me as they do.
- I would miss out on the sex.
- I can't open up to anyone else.
- If I leave, then I'm alone.

Reasons for Incentives:

- They love me.
- They are intimate with me.
- We have fun together.
- We love each other.
- They give me whatever I want.
- They're perfect.

As you can see this model describes factors that can cause commitment in a relationship as you need to invest in a relationship for commitment to form.

CHAPTER 8: WHY RELATIONSHIPS CHANGE AND END?

Such an interesting question, isn't it?

Because sometimes it's easy to understand why a relationship breaks down but other times it's harder to understand why.

Although some common reasons include:

- Cheating
- Changes in personality
- Not seeing them enough
- Arguments
- And many, many more…

In addition, several external influences that could cause a relationship to end.

External influences are influences that occur outside the relationship. For example: if a group of people don't like you being friends with someone, and they spread rumours and they do everything in their power to kill the friendship.

That's a personal example of external influences.

Rollie and Duck:

In 2006, they did a longitudinal study of couples as well as they formulated five stages of relationship breakdown. They are:

- Intrapsychic stage- where upset is experienced by one or both parties and not told to the other.

- Dyadic stage- partners voice their concerns and upset and depending on attribution styles this is resolved or avoided.

- Social stage- partners seek support and share their concerns with the wide community.

- Grave dressing- stories are prepared in order to save face and partner defends their decision to break up.

- Resurrection- partners recover and redefine what they want in a relationship.

Other studies support this model as well. Adding creditability and reliability to the model.

LeFebvre, Blackburn and Brody (2014):

226 college students completed an online survey about relationships that had ended in the past two years. They rated the seriousness of the relationship and communication patterns pre, during and post-breakup.

Results showed that people in the during relationship dissolution stage deleted and aim to wipe out traces of their partner. By: deleting wall postings and their online relationship status and by blocking and unfriending people.

During the post-dissolution stage- people continue to wipe out traces of their former partner but impression management behaviour increases with the aim of increasing jealousy or regret from previous partners.

In conclusion, these findings support the Rollie and Duck (2006) model. Especially, the last three stages: social stage, grave dressing and resurrection.

Critical Thinking:

This study has high temporal validity because the study was done recently so we know that the results can be applied to the world today, as the study was done recently.

However, the results of the study could be false

in a sense because the participant could have lied on the questionnaires to save face; if they had been horrible to their ex over the breakup; to conform to social expectations. Due to the participant could have done something that could be deemed odd because of the breakup. For example, they could have cyberstalked their ex to try and win them back or bombarded them with messages.

Overall, some of the study's results could be tainted by these or similar reasons so it's possible that the trend isn't as clear cut in reality as the study suggests.

Flora and Segrin (2003):

65 married couples and 66 dating couples took part in relationship stability measurements twice with a 6-month interval.

Semi-structured interviews were used to answer open-ended questions on a topic like affection and negativity towards the partner.

Relationship development breadth was assessed as well through a questionnaire which assessed the extent to which different behaviours were experienced by the couples. Like: feeling a deep emotional connection and sexual intimacy.

Results showed that breakup and lower satisfactory six months after the study was related to little relation breadth and negative interviews.

In conclusion- a variety of behavioural, cognitive and affective experiences are needed for a long-lasting relationship.

Critical Thinking:

A positive of the study was that they used more than one research method in the experiment. This, in turn, creates more data for them to use in their results and increase the reliability of their findings as well as conclusions as they can support it with more data.

However, the relationship breath test could be flawed as it could be open to demand characteristics. This is where the participants write down or do what they think the experimenters want them to do. Therefore, some of the data could not reflect what the couples are like in the real world.

In this case, it would be the participant stating that they had a shallow breath at the begin of the six months and then stating that they have a very wide breath at the end of the six months.

PART THREE: PROSOCIAL BEHAVIOUR

CHAPTER 9: BYSTANDERISM

In this chapter, the studies will talk more about Bystanderism than me, but it will be interesting.

Bystanderism is also known as the Bystander Effect is when someone is less likely to help if there are other people around.

The Bystander Effect, I do find interesting because why do people not help when you can clearly see that someone needs help.

In everyday life, there are thousands of examples of the Bystander Effect.

Here are only a few examples and I bet that all of us would like to think we would help but, in reality, I bet none of us would help, or only the best of us would.

- You see a man being chased down the street by a group of three men who look intimidating or threatening. The man being chased clearly needs help and is terrified for his life.

• You're stuck in traffic and you see an old lady walking past with heavy shopping bags, and you know that she's going to fall.

• You're on a busy train and you see a young girl getting bullied by a group of mean girls.

And there are thousands of more examples demonstrating the Bystander Effect.

Personally, I find it interesting because as a society we are bred to be helpful and the best we can but when it comes to it. Barely any of us are actually helpful to complete strangers.

For the case studies, I'll do a combined critical thinking section.

Darley and Latane (1968):

Psychology students took part in a conversation with other students over an intercom system.

Round 1 each participant was to present their problems. Round 2 was to comment on what other people had said and round 3 was for free discussion.

In reality, all other people heard over the intercom system were recordings.

The future victim spoke first in the discussion tell them that it was hard to adjust to the new city and he was prone to seizures under stress.

In round 2, he started to have a seizure and asked for help then went quiet.

Then the subject was timed to see if they went to find help and after being debriefed, they filled in a series of questionnaires.

Results showed that the number of bystanders does increase the response time as when it was the victim and subject 85% responded to the emergency and it took an average of 52 seconds to respond.

Whereas only 31% of people responded when it was them, the victim and four other people with it taking them on average of 166 seconds.

In conclusion, the subjects were in conflict about whether or not to help because they didn't want to overreact and destroy the experiment but equally they didn't want the shame of not helping. This can be explained by diffusion of responsibility as with their being more people there were more people for the responsibility to psychologically distributed.

Latane and Darley (1968)

Students were placed into three groups and all were asked to fill out a questionnaire and after a while, the room began to fill with smoke.

One group was when the participant was in the room alone.

Group two was when the participant was in the room with two other people. These people were asked to act indifferent and ignore the smoke.

The last condition was when the participant was in the room with two other participants.

Results showed that when alone 75% of the participant reported the smoke.

When with two other people only 10% reported the smoke and when in condition 3 only 38% reported the smoke.

In interviews, participant thought the smoke was strange but wasn't sure if it was dangerous.

In conclusion, when faced with an ambiguous situation people tend to rely on the reactions of others and are influenced by them. This can lead them to interpret the event as not dangerous and a phenomenon known as pluralistic ignorance.

Critical Thinking:

While both studies were effectively controlled as they both had several experimental groups so we could see the effects of Bystanderism in different contexts as well as with several different numbers.

Both studies lacked ecological validity because if we take the intercom study for instance. In a real-world situation, you can see other people's expressions to a situation and these expressions amongst other things play a role in deciding whether to help or not. Therefore, this could affect the results because this could have led to an increase in the response time or a decrease.

CHAPTER 10: WHY PEOPLE DON'T HELP?

In the last chapter, we looked at the Bystander Effect and three factors behind Bystanderism.

So, in this chapter, I wanted to investigate the topic of why people don't help in more depth because Bystanderism isn't the answer to everything.

Rationality of Not Helping:

To answer this question, Bickman (1972) ran a study where the participants were led to believe they were in an experiment with two other participants/confederates.

Subsequently, the participants heard a bookcase fall on top of one of the confederates, and the participants believed the other confederate could or couldn't help the person.

Also, they heard the other confederate interpret

the event as an accident or not.

In short, as a participant would have heard the bookcase fall on another person and if it was an accident or not, as well as if you were needed to help rescue the person.

The results showed participants were a lot more likely to help if the confederate deemed it to be a definite emergency and they couldn't help them.

This makes sense because if someone is trapped; it wasn't urgent and you weren't needed to help. Chances are you aren't going to help because you're not needed.

And yes, I can hear the numbers of readers saying "Yes I would still help,"

I agree I want to think that but chances are we won't.

When Do Numbers of Bystanders Increase Helping?

I quite like the study below because in psychology we hear a lot about the negative sides of social group (Social Psychology 3rd Edition) and the Bystander Effect.

Therefore, I always love studies that turn the current research consensus on its head.

Since we think the number of Bystanders only

decrease helping, but it can increase helping in certain situations.

Greilemeyer & Mugge (2015) conducted an experiment where they told students they needed 1 or 4 people to do an experiment. As well as the participants believed they were alone or 10 other people that received the request.

The hypothesises were:

- If one person is needed the number of bystanders should decrease helping as supported by Latane & Darley (1968)
- When others are needed, the more bystanders there are, there should be an increase in helping.

Their results showed the participants thought helping made 'less sense' when one person was needed but many were available. As well as when many were needed and only 1 was available.

This was caused by the diffusion of responsibility in the first scenario.

Whereas when the opposite was true when many people were needed, and many were available. This increased helping.

Again, I think this study has a lot of real-world applications because if multiple people are needed to help. Then what's the point of one person trying?

Also, I would love to think that I would still try and chances are I probably would. Yet it is still interesting to consider.

A Final Study:

Lastly, Harari, Harari & White (1985) studied rape scenario on a university campus to see if men alone or men in groups would help.

The results showed men in groups overwhelming helped. Probably due to feeling safe and the norm is to help.

Critical Thinking:

Nonetheless, the study was far from perfect because helping is naturally strong in a natural setting. Since humans are inclined to help others.

You'll see in the next chapter on Altruism how true that can be sometimes.

Additionally, there was no discussion of ethics in the study because these weren't briefed, and informed consent wasn't obtained before the study.

Furthermore, when someone cries rape, you know its an emergency so the generalisability of the findings might not be as high as you think it is.

Due to the results of the study can only be generalised to situations that are clearly an emergency.

On the positive side, participants who thought they would have to talk to the participant later helped faster.

In addition, the number of confederates had no impact on this. (Gottlieb & Carver, 1980)

Lastly and perhaps the most interesting finding is public self-awareness reverses The Bystander Effect.

I talk a lot more about self-awareness in Social Psychology. Yet I think this is an interesting finding as it could mean the way to get more people to help others, could be to make them more aware of themselves in these situations.

Since if people know they're being watched, and let's face it judged by others, for their actions then it might make more people help others.

For example, if a person was walking in a street and they saw an elderly lady fall over and no one, including the elderly woman saw that person, then there's a chance they would avoid the situation, and hope someone else would help.

However, if that person thought about the negative judgements other people would be giving them for not helping. Then maybe, just maybe they would help.

It's an interesting idea to think about.

CHAPTER 11: ALTRUISM

Prosocial behaviour is an interesting topic in psychology because it's difficult to say why human show the behaviour. Especially, when we show altruistic behaviour.

This behaviour is when we help others even when the behaviour could harm us.

For example, let's say you're walking through your street and you see a gang of people with knives beating up a stranger, and it's clear that the stranger will die without your help, and you run over to help the stranger. Even if it could result in your death.

That's altruistic behaviour.

Yet WHY do it? When there is such a high risk of danger and it goes against many psychological rules.

Such as evolutionary theory states that we

wouldn't help because it would threaten the chance of us reproducing and passing on our genes to the next generation, so it goes against evolutionary theory.

Thus, psychologists are divided on the why of this particular behaviour.

As some believe that we show altruism for egotistical reasons. For example, you would attack the gang so you could feel good about yourself and you become a local hero. Increasing your social status in the local community.

Then other psychologists believe that humans are capable of true altruism, so you helped that stranger because you just wanted to. It was the right thing to do.

Personally, I'm more cynical so I believe in the egotistical reason.

What Factors Can Determine If Altruism Occurs?

- Personality and situational factors can increase helping. For instance, if you have a helpful personality then you are more likely to help others as well as if the situation promotes helping then you are more likely to help. One example could be if others are helping then you are more likely to help in that situation compared to a situation where everyone is simply walking past. (See Bystanderism for more information)

- Machvavellism is the willingness to manipulate others for gain. As excepted as Machvavellism increase, helping behaviour decreases.
- Belief in a just world- generally the belief in a just world is likely to prevent people from doing wrong or failing in moral duties. (Hafer, 2000; Sutton and Winnard, 2007) However, these beliefs can increase the chance of people not helping when they don't feel obligated to help. (Balbert, 1999; Stelan and Sutton,2011)
- Empathy- as excepted the more empathy a person has the more likely they are to help someone.
- Moral reasoning- people who reason more tend to demonstrate a higher level of empathy and altruism.
- Religiosity- if you're religious and if your religion promotes helping others then you are more likely to people to serve your god or Faith.

However, this isn't always true because if you would insult or offend your religion by helping a particular someone. Then you are less unlikely to help someone. For example, if it's an extremely devoted Christian than helping a gay person would be unthinkable since they're a sinner.

- Having positive role models- Scloeder, Penner, Dovido and Pilivin (1995) showed that people who witness more altruistic behaviour from role models tend to be more altruistic themselves.
- Similarity- if the person who needs help is like you then you are more likely to help them.
- Culture- as collective cultures focus more on the needs of the group, they are more likely to help than individualistic cultures. (See Social Psychology for more information)

When it comes to helping behaviour there are certain characteristics that can increase the chance of being helped. For instance:

- Age- the younger you are the more likely it is that people will help you. This could be linked to evolution as the young are more fertile so by saving them we are increasing the likelihood of them reproducing and ensuring the survival of the species.
- Gender- woman are more likely to receive help than men. (Bruder- Maltson and Hovanitz, 1990)
- Attractiveness- the more attractive you are the more likely it is that you will be helped (Witson and Dovidio, 1985)

Kin-selection Theory:

This theory was proposed by Hamilton (1964) as an extension of evolutionary theory and he stated that we help others to increase the chances of our genetic material being passed on.

So according to the theory:

- Relatives will be the target for helping behaviour as they will have more of our genetic behaviour than other people.
- Closer relatives would be helped more than distant ones as they will have more of our genetic material.
- Healthier and younger people would be helped more as they are more likely to reproduce and pass on the genetic material.

However, I personally must highlight a few problems with this theory:

- How can humans detect genetic material in strangers?
- Why do humans help complete strangers?
- Why do humans help elderly or infertile people as they won't be able to pass on genetic material?
- Finally, why do humans help homosexuals as they are unlikely to pass on their genetic material?

If the theory can answer those questions, then I'll

probably believe in the theory a bit more.

Madsen et al (2007):

UK students and South African Zulu were asked to provide a list of genetic variable people. Like: mother, siblings and grandparents.

Then they were asked to take up a painful position like sitting on a chair with your back against the wall and legs and tights at right angles.

They were asked to hold the position for as long as possible and time equalled a payment; £1.50 for 20 seconds for UK students and food hampers for the Zulu people; for the recipient. There were five trials in total each for a different person. Like: themselves, mother, brother, cousin and a local charity.

Results showed that subjects were more prepared to maintain the position for people they were related to. For example, they held it for longer for themselves over their parents.

This was transcultural.

In conclusion, kinship plays a role in moderating autistic behaviour.

Critical thinking:

While, this experiment was a cross-cultural study, so we know that the behaviour is a part of the behavioural trend and possibly universal.

The study has low ecological validity as in the real world I doubt this situation would ever be used or happen. Therefore, it's questionable about whether we can apply the findings to the real world given how artificial this scenario was.

Empathy-Altruism Hypothesis:

Batson et al's theory states that people help others have real concern and if another person has empathy for another then they will help.

As I said though, I'm cynical so I have complete faith in this theory, not.

Batson et al (1981):

44 female psychology students took part in a 2x2 experiment involving them going into a room and watching a recording of Elaine who was being shocked at random intervals. From the first shock, it was clear she found them very unpleasant.

From the second trial out of ten, the subject was allowed to help her by taking her place.

The IV that made up the groups were: easy vs difficult escape wherein the difficult escape they believed that if they didn't help her they would have to continue to watch the situation.

In the easy escape condition, they believed they could just walk away.

Low vs high level of empathy- this was done by everyone completing a questionnaire on values and believes and Elaine's was done beforehand then her questionnaire was shown to the subject so they could know if Elaine was similar or not to them. As the study claimed that increased similarity means increased empathy towards the person.

The results showed:
- Easy escape/low empathy condition- 18%
- Easy escape/ high empathy- 91%
- Difficult escape/low empathy- 64%
- Difficult escape/ high empathy

In conclusion, when the level of empathy was high the desire to help was altruism not egoistic and ease of escape no longer had an effect when the level of empathy was high.

Critical Thinking:

While this study has strong internal validity as it effectively measured what it intended to.

It does have several ethical concerns as the students weren't protected against the possible psychological harm and deceit used in the experiment.

CHAPTER 12: PAROCHIAL ALTRUISM

In the last chapter, we looked at Altruism and I introduced you to the topic, so in this chapter, I want to go into this topic in more depth by looking at Parochial Altruism.

In essences, this is all about intragroup social dilemmas and when people to pool together and sacrifice their own interests for the sake of the group.

Although, a more professional and horrible definition is:

Parochial altruism is the propensity for people to engage in behaviour that would cost them **to** protect group members from the outgroup.

Moving from that horrible definition, co-operation between people is against the interest of the self but in the interest of the group.

For example, if we look at some real-life social

dilemmas. We can see that soldiers at war are costly to the individual soldiers, but they can greatly benefit the group.

Another real-life example is environmental behaviours because if we take the example of being a vegetarian. This costs the self since they aren't able to enjoy meat but they're supporting sustainable eating and they're decreasing their carbon footprint. This benefits all of humanity.

Another example would be team sports like football or rugby because they're potentially dangerous to the players. Yet the concept of victory, especially at international events, means they benefit the group. In this case, it would be benefiting the winning country.

Finally, a great example that applies to most people will be paying tax. Due to paying tax costs people money, sometimes a lot of it, but without paying tax. We wouldn't have a lot of the things, we take for granted.

That's the reason why I support paying tax, but I hate VAT. Because it tends to make some online courses for me a bit more expensive.

Types of Social Dilemmas:

If we look into this type of altruism in more depth, we need to know that social dilemmas are an umbellar term with a number of types.

For example, there are public good dilemmas where people cannot be prevented from using a resource, so the individual is better off if they don't contribute.

This is a difficult type to find examples for but it could be argued eating meat and using non-renewable electricity is certainly one of these types of resources.

Another type of dilemmas is the Common Dilemma. If you get a chance look into the geography topic of the Tragedy of the Commons, it's an interesting idea.

Anyway, this is where everyone has access to the resource but if overused nobody will have access to it.

You don't need to be too creative with examples here because examples include fossil fuels, public parks (I did a news feature of this topic on The Psychology World Podcast) and anything else that is not renewable.

Ruthlessness:

To conclude this chapter on Parochial Altruism, I think it's interesting if we talk about the fact humans are more ruthless for us than we.

In other words, we are more ruthless to others when it's for us compared to an ingroup.

This is known as "interindividual- intergroup ferocity" as well as it was proposed by Wildschut et al (2003)

According to the paper, there are a few reasons why people are more ruthless. For example, fear is one factor because it's assumed groups are competitive with one another. (Campbell, 1967, Universal Outgroup Stereotype)

Another factor is greed because usually ruthlessness is inhibited by group norms but group members can justify ruthlessness since it encourages competitive intergroup behaviour. (Insko et al, 1990)

Additionally, this feeds into the idea that this allows group members to rationalize ruthless because in other words group members can say "I'm not being selfish. I'm doing it for the group"

However, this is only the case when people are not already prone to guilt because you're hardly going to be ruthless and horrible to people if you're going to feel guilty later.

Lastly, ruthlessness is believed to have a biological/ evolutionary basis to defend our own social groups. As well as this can be tested by looking at Oxytocin.

This is an important hormone that is associated with trust, affiliation and other important social processes.

I highly recommend checking out Romeo (2014)'s study on oxytocin. You can find that in Biological Psychology.

CHAPTER 13: SOCIAL IDENTIFICATION AND THE DARK SIDE OF ALTRUISM

Moving into hardcore social psychology and I really encourage you to read Social Psychology for more depth. The more people identify with a group, the more they are likely to co-operate.

This is especially true if people are pro-self. (De Cremer & Van Vugt, 1999)

These people focus on getting resources for themselves, and some pro-self people proactively attempt to make sure others get fewer resources than themselves.

That's bad!

Whereas pro-social people focus on getting resources for the group so everyone can benefit.

Consequently, when pro-self and pro-social

people played a problem goods dilemma fame, but their social identification was manipulated.

The results showed pro-self people donated more money when there was high group identification.

In other words, people are more willing to help others when they are a part of the same social group.

Is Altruism Always Nice?

At first, it would seem like people doing Altruism is always for the betterment of people.

However, people often punish defectors at their own expense. This is called: altruistic punishment (Fehr & Gachter, 2002)

Altruistic punishment:

Fehr & Gachter (2002) created the term and they argued that evolution, moreover group selection predispose us to punish free-riders.

This I can fully understand because I hate free riders as I want everyone to contribute. Even though, when I'm in a group I end up doing all the work most of the time.

Furthermore, Fehr & Gachter (2002) ran an experiment using public good dilemmas in a round of 6 blocks, where participants were allowed to punish defectors om some blocks.

The results showed 84% of people punished at least 1 defector.

Meaning we are more than willing to take part in altruistic punishment and harm ourselves and others given the chance for our social group.

CHAPTER 14: PROMOTING PROSOCIAL BEHAVIOUR

On the last chapter of our human relationship journey, there isn't much theory in truth but there should always exist factors that decrease the Bystander Effect and make a society that actively helps each other.

Some ways to do this include:

- A system of incentives- these incentives decrease the cost of helping and increase the cost of not helping.

- Targeting psychological variables- these schemes teach people skills associated with prosocial behaviour or they trained people typically young people to be more responsive to the needs of other people.

Nguyen and Parker (2018):

Good Samaritan laws are designed to protect people who show prosocial behaviour even if people get hurt as a result of their actions. Examples of these laws are in Canada, Argentina and Australia.

In the USA, drug-related deaths are the highest causes of deaths, therefore, more and more states are adopting laws that protect people from prosecuting if they experience or witness a drug overdose and call emergency services.

To test the effectiveness, the study analysed 270 hospital admissions in New York and New Jersey before and after the law was adopted.
Results show that there was an increase in heroin-related admissions but not in non-heroin related admissions.

Therefore, the law is effective at increasing heroin-related admissions.

Critical thinking:

This study effectively shows how these laws can increase hospital admissions so this, in turn, promotes prosocial behaviour. However, as only the heroin-related admissions increased can we really say that these laws are completely effective. As if they were very effectively then surely all drug-related admissions would be up instead of only heroin-related admissions?

Hutcherson, Seppala and Gross (2008):

93 volunteers who rarely or never meditated in their daily life.

They were split into two groups: a guided 7-minute love-kindness mediation and neutral imagery induction.

They tested their explicit and implicit responses before and after their session to six photos.

To test explicit responses a 7-point system was used to ask each subject how they connected and how positive they felt towards the image.

To test implicit responses, each photo was shown randomly 18 times followed by a positive and a negative word. Then they needed to quickly say if the word was positive or negative. The implicit responses were shown by a bias for a type of words.

Results showed love-kindness mediation was best for increasing social connection and positivity towards strangers in explicit and implicit responses.

In conclusion, this easy technique may help to decrease social isolation, but further research must be done to see if these results are short term or long term.

Critical thinking:

This was a well-controlled study as the experiment got two groups to compare and they tested implicit and explicit responses, so they had a lot of data to support their conclusions.

Nevertheless, without a longitudinal study being completed we can't say with any real evidence that the effects of this mediation are long term or short term. Therefore, more research must be done in this area.

BIBLIOGRAPHY

Lee Parker (author), Darren Seath (author) Alexey Popov (author), *Oxford IB Diploma Programme: Psychology Course Companion,* 2nd edition, OUP Oxford, 2017

Alexey Popov, *IB Psychology Study Guide: Oxford IB Diploma Programme,* 2nd edition, OUP Oxford, 2018

Sutton, R.M., & Douglas, K.M. (2013). Social psychology. Basingstoke, UK: Palgrave MacMillan

Thank you for reading.

I hoped you enjoyed it.

If you want a FREE book and keep up to date about new books and project. Then please sign up for my newsletter at www.connorwhiteley.net/

Have a great day.

CHECK OUT THE PSYCHOLOGY WORLD PODCAST FOR MORE PSYCHOLOGY INFORMATION!

AVAILABLE ON ALL MAJOR PODCAST APPS.

CONNOR WHITELEY

About the author:

Connor Whiteley is the author of over 20 books in the sci-fi fantasy, nonfiction psychology and books for writer's genre and he is a Human Branding Speaker and Consultant.

He is a passionate warhammer 40,000 reader, psychology student and author.

Who narrates his own audiobooks and he hosts The Psychology World Podcast.

All whilst studying Psychology at the University of Kent, England.

Also, he was a former Explorer Scout where he gave a speech to the Maltese President in August 2018 and he attended Prince Charles' 70th Birthday Party at Buckingham Palace in May 2018.

Plus, he is a self-confessed coffee lover!

Please follow me on:

Website: www.connorwhiteley.net

Twitter: @scifiwhiteley

Please leave on honest review as this helps with the discoverability of the book and I truly appreciate it.

Thank you for reading. I hope you've enjoyed.

All books in 'An Introductory Series':

BIOLOGICAL PSYCHOLOGY 3RD EDITION

COGNITIVE PSYCHOLOGY 2ND EDITION

SOCIAL PSYCHOLOGY- 3RD EDITION

ABNORMAL PSYCHOLOGY 3RD EDITION

PSYCHOLOGY OF RELATIONSHIPS- 3RD EDITION

DEVELOPMENTAL PSYCHOLOGY 3RD EDITION

HEALTH PSYCHOLOGY

RESEARCH IN PSYCHOLOGY

A GUIDE TO MENTAL HEALTH AND TREATMENT AROUND THE WORLD- A GLOBAL LOOK AT DEPRESSION

FORENSIC PSYCHOLOGY

CLINICAL PSYCHOLOGY

FORMULATION IN PSYCHOTHERAPY

Other books by Connor Whiteley:

WINTER'S REVENGE

WINTER'S DISSENSION

<u>Companion guides:</u>

BIOLOGICAL PSYCHOLOGY 2ND EDITION WORKBOOK

COGNITIVE PSYCHOLOGY 2ND EDITION WORKBOOK

SOCIOCULTURAL PSYCHOLOGY 2ND EDITION WORKBOOK

ABNORMAL PSYCHOLOGY 2ND EDITION WORKBOOK

PSYCHOLOGY OF HUMAN RELATIONSHIPS 2ND EDITION WORKBOOK

HEALTH PSYCHOLOGY WORKBOOK

FORENSIC PSYCHOLOGY WORKBOOK

Audiobooks by Connor Whiteley:

BIOLOGICAL PSYCHOLOGY

COGNITIVE PSYCHOLOGY

SOCIOCULTURAL PSYCHOLOGY

ABNORMAL PSYCHOLOGY

PSYCHOLOGY OF HUMAN
RELATIONSHIPS

HEALTH PSYCHOLOGY

DEVELOPMENTAL PSYCHOLOGY

RESEARCH IN PSYCHOLOGY

FORENSIC PSYCHOLOGY

GARRO: GALAXY'S END

GARRO: RISE OF THE ORDER

GARRO: SHORT STORIES

GARRO: END TIMES

GARRO: COLLECTION

GARRO: HERESY

GARRO: FAITHLESS

GARRO: DESTROYER OF WORLDS

GARRO: COLLECTION BOOKS 4-6

GARRO: COLLECTION BOOKS 1-6

Business books:

TIME MANAGEMENT: A GUIDE FOR STUDENTS AND WORKERS

LEADERSHIP: WHAT MAKES A GOOD LEADER? A GUIDE FOR STUDENTS AND WORKERS.

BUSINESS SKILLS: HOW TO SURVIVE THE BUSINESS WORLD? A GUIDE FOR STUDENTS, EMPLOYEES AND EMPLOYERS.

BUSINESS COLLECTION

GET YOUR FREE BOOK AT:

WWW.CONNORWHITELEY.NET

Lightning Source UK Ltd.
Milton Keynes UK
UKHW021855040521
383144UK00004B/503